THE SMART HOUSE

THE SMA

ART HOUSE

by James Grayson Trulove

introduction by
Michael McDonough

Title page: Lexon/MacCarthy Residence, Lorcan O'Herlihy Architects
Tom Bonner, Photographer

Copyright© 2002 by James Grayson Trulove and HDI, an imprint of
HarperCollins Publishers

Published in 2003 by
Harper Design International, an imprint of
HarperCollins Publishers
10 East 53rd Street
New York, New York 10022-5299

Distributed throughout the world by
HarperCollins International
10 East 53rd Street
New York, New York 10022-5299
Fax: (212) 207-7654

ISBN: 0-06-055742-7

Packaged by:
Grayson Publishing
1250 28th Street NW
Washington, D.C. 20007
Tel: (202) 337-1380
Fax: (202) 337-1381

Printed in Hong Kong
First Printing, 2003

2 3 4 5 6 7 8 9 /04 03

CONTENTS

The Smart House Examined

By Michael McDonough

eft, the e-House started as a series of digital images and textural information posted at www.e-house2000.com - a dedi-
ated project website. The project team and its research and development components were developed through this site
nd its e-mail links; the same site will control the completed house and its systems.

Smart house technology came into focus with the advent of the Internet and, while increasingly

ophisticated, is for the most part still in its developmental stages. The organizing idea here—that a

uilding or a system can be automated to supervise and perform certain managerial tasks -- is not new.

ou can go see automated manufacturing facilities, power plants, remotely located utility lines, shop-

ing malls, high rise structures, and other large, complex areas of human endeavor. These things are

xpensive to maintain and difficult to control, so automation is a critical factor in any economic efficien-

y model developed to manage them. With automation, essentially smart building technology, fewer

ersonnel could be employed, security could be enhanced, accidents could be reduced, and money

ould be saved. Existing communications networks could be employed. Smart technology was efficient. It made good business sense. It got put into big buildings and infrastructures.

But to get it into your home was something different, something new. Standard business categories really did not apply to the average homeowner who ostensibly just wanted things to be a bit simpler to run. It was not really about economic incentives or existing communications infrastructure.

It was about convenience.

The driving force behind smart house technology in its earliest phases has been convenience. Convenience for the home user, who–it was assumed–would be motivated to lessen the time required for certain repetitive tasks and mundane chores. These might include interior lighting, as in lowering the lights for a social gathering or raising them so that the premises could be cleaned after the guests had left. Similarly, entertainment systems would be pre-programmed and centrally managed. One's favorite disco tracks could be pre-selected, and distributed to the living room and den in the house, while being kept out of the children's rooms. Security—seen in part as an offshoot of convenience— could also be addressed, so that the home owner would have a smart house system check the status of all doors and windows, make sure that motion sensors were armed, and that the system was capable of reporting problems to whomever was deemed most appropriate.

Any and all of these and related categories could be taken to higher levels of sophistication, where window blinds could be raised or lowered remotely, heating systems could be turned on from a hundred miles away, yard lighting could be automated, and surveillance camera technology could be implemented. The fullest manifestation of this would be the "integrated house," where all the systems, everything that was wired, would be controllable from a central location running a centralized control panel. You could raise and lower the shades while selecting a lighting setting and arming the security system.

Convenience would—it was assumed—drive the market, and smart house technology would be a selling point in new house sales. The Internet—just starting to blossom—would function as a communications pipeline. Eventually everyone would want the stuff, and a golden age of automated ease would dawn.

Smart.or not quite so smart?

Several countervailing forces emerged, and as surely as childhood innocence yields to adolescent rebellion, the smart house became more like—as the New York Times reported it—the Smart Alec house. It got complicated. Houses had to be wired or networked, control panels had to be installed, passwords had to be logged, protocols had to be learned. Something might "glitch," and a repair person would have to be called. A password might get lost. The remote control might get lost. Maybe the software manual was misplaced. Or you couldn't remember the 22-digit registration number so you were in the tech support dead zone on hold for three hours. Maybe a power outage or spike would blow the system's brains out and you would have to start again. Or, maybe, just maybe, the dot.com

Right, the first floor of e-House has a great room with a high-efficiency wood-burning fireplace, kitchen, and living-dining area. Ancillary spaces include a small office, lavatory, and "light catcher" stair with garden.

Below right, the second floor is a mezzanine with room for future second office or bedroom, a master bedroom and bathroom. The "view catcher" faces north to the principal views on the site.

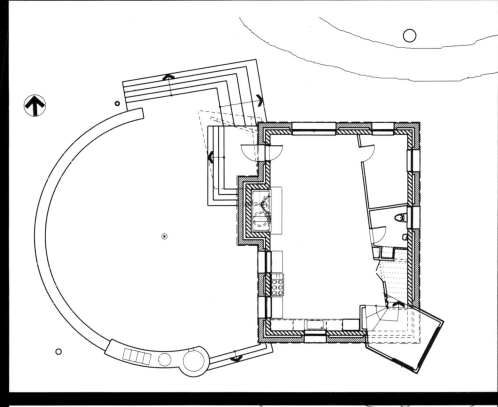

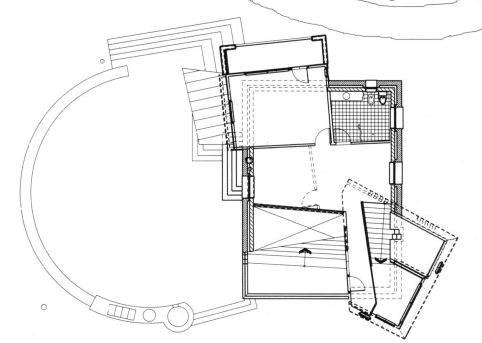

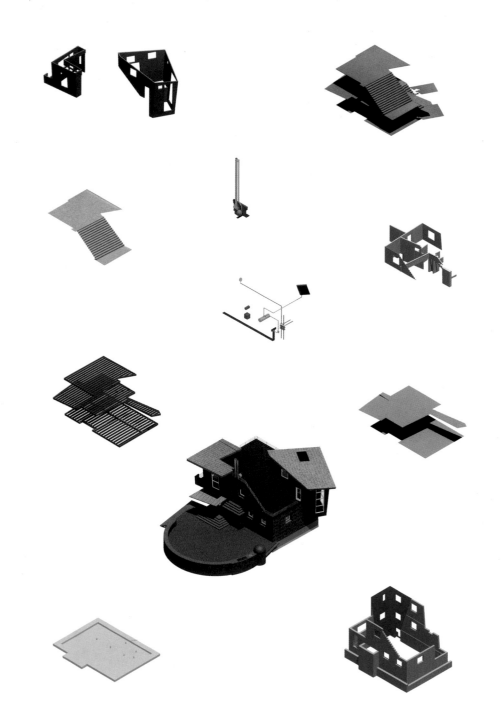

Above, the e-House2000 employs dozens of new and alternative green technologies, from its future-proofed subsurface data cabling to its thermally efficient building envelope, healthy home interior finishes, and high-tech zinc coated roofing. All were sourced on the Internet.

entity that sold you the system was in Chapter 11 and no longer available to help. The Garrison Colonial with the tennis court and pool with the high IQ was having a temper tantrum, and you couldn't necessarily reason with it.

This was not convenience. It was inconvenience with a high price tag and a service contract tacked on. Initially enthusiastic, now those high-end home owners were reporting that they would try use the smart house system once or twice, then give up on it. They would never bother programming the software. Or they would not repair the system if it broke down. It was the stuff of suburban support groups.

No matter, said the industry, the motivated homeowner will still bite for the luxury implicit in the thing, and the big developers who market gated communities see smart house technology as a value-added item, and they will pretty much go for it anyway. And the so industry pushes on.

New technologies in the pipeline include the much vaunted refrigerator that constantly surveys its own contents, then tells you when to buy more milk. And the motion-activated camera that tracks the live-alones, the impaired, and the aged so that their every move can be noted and evaluated, and so that medical personnel can be summoned in the event of an emergency. One might say of this brave new wired world, "great."

One might also say, however, that I am sick of milk and would like to try soy bean drinks or a beer for a change. Or that if my whole darn life has become so regimented that the refrigerator can order me around, and I will be tracked while sitting on the toilet just in case I fall off, well, then, upon mature consideration, I'd rather be dead. So label me DNR, and let me pass with a modicum of dignity.

Luddite, I? Not at all. Quite to the contrary, I am a techie, and pretty die-hard at that. I believe firmly that smart house technology will continue to be an important part of new house design and construction, that it will be part of home renovation markets, that it will provide new and amazing services to the home owner, and that it will continue to evolve with the Internet and other networking technologies. I like the smart house. And I am building my own version in upstate New York. It is called "e-House2000" and will have all sorts of smart technologies, but–and herein lies the rub–they are not based on convenience.

Like the power plants and manufacturing assembly lines, the e-House is based on that good old business model war-horse, efficiency. Energy efficiency is the raison d'être of the thing, but it doesn't stop there. Home repairs are anticipated and called-in before they become critical. The pathway to my door has a snow melt system that turns itself on when snow is first predicted so that snow and ice can never accumulate. Power failures are a thing of the past because an uninterruptable power system

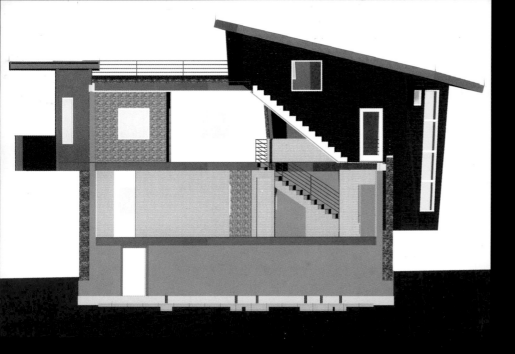

Left, a longitudinal section showing interior construction. The large trapezoidal "light catcher" allows the first light of dawn to penetrate deep into the interior, and houses a stairway and indoor garden. Cantilevered so that it literally reaches outward to the light, it also provides computer monitored daylighting all year-round.

(UPS) sits watching the house. Load-shedding software makes sure that big, energy hog appliances (bossy refrigerators and computer monitors) can't draw-down the back-up systems. My water quality is monitored. And the blinds are raised because here comes a big batch of passive solar sunlight at the first crack of dawn, and we can use that to light the house and warm the floors.

The key words here are, once again, whole house integration, but with a sort of vengeance. The e-House2000 project began as a website (www-ehouse2000.com), a place where the building was designed, where fabulous sustainable technologies were evaluated and designed-in, and where the building morphed into a structure that maximized its potential efficiencies and wonderments before ground was broken. This was not about integration of the control systems within themselves, but integration of the control systems into the building design and vice versa. It is as if the house both breathes and monitors its own breathing for maximum well-being.

In e-House, the building knows when to raise the blinds not because it's easier, but in order to catch the rising sun. And the special two-stories-high windows that hold the blinds face east-southeast to capture those precious first rays, and because you need to jump-start the solar warming cycle first thing in the morning. If the super-efficient fireplace warms the great room, the radiant heat zone there will tamp itself down automatically. And if the thermal solar collectors are making more hot water than the house can use, the excess will be routed to a special storage area that holds hot water for showers, heat for snow melt, or heat exchange for air conditioning. Sensors will monitor indoor air quality

Right, the e-House2000 is configured to "catch" views of a park-like meadow to the north and harvest maximal solar energy and light. The trapezoidal cantilevered "view catcher" was computer-designed in response to solar angle and shading, rendered here with the last rays of winter solstice light at its western side.

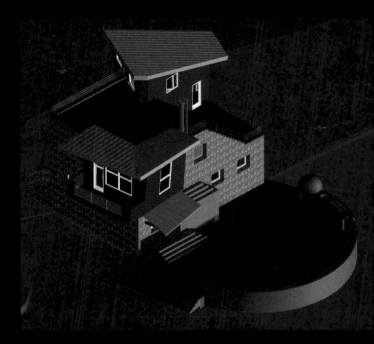

humidity, condensation, and other health and well-being criteria, then adjust the air flow and filtration levels accordingly. Outdoor fresh air, when it is fresh enough, will be circulated. The original website continues, now as a data collection site, and a place to check in and see if everything is as it should be.

In essence, the smart house is also a healthy house: a smart place to be. It will save you operating costs. It will never have sick building syndrome. It will water the plants when no one is around. You can still listen to the audio system in every room, but you can also turn on the dishwasher from Tokyo, and know that if a circuit-breaker pops or the power lines snap under the strain of an ice storm, the refrigerator will still be running.

Sound far-fetched? All of the hardware and software you need to construct these systems, to make a really smart house, a building that works like a money-grubbing, self-regulating, comfort addicted, integrated organism, already exist. You can find the technology on the Internet (I did). You can purchase it with a credit card and have it overnighted to an address of your choosing. And the technology is relatively "bulletproof" because it has been out there running big structures and systems for years. Some of it even updates and repairs itself. The next phase of smart building is, in essence, very adult, lying around waiting to be picked up and made use of.

So the question might be, if all the technology we need is out there, is it really the house that needs to get smart?

SMART TECHNOLOGY

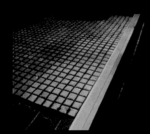

Beleuchtung	Essgeschoss
Fenster	Wohngeschoss
Bewässerung	Schlafgeschoss
Klima	Erdgeschoss
Abwesend	Gästehaus
	Eingang
	Garten

Beenden · Windows

Kamera · Schließen

This four-level residence is sited on a steep parcel of land in

Stuttgart, Germany. Access is via a bridge leading to the top floor.

This level accommodates the kitchen and dining area and the next

two levels contain living and sleeping areas, respectively. The bot-

tom level has a nursery and houses mechanical components.

Each of the four floors is defined by a few pieces of carefully selected

furniture, reflecting the minimalist, transparent quality of the exterior

of the building.

The house is a modular design and it is constructed entirely of glass with no internal partitions. The load-bearing structure of the building consists of a steel frame stiffened by diagonal members and erected on a reinforced concrete slab. The floors are heavy-sectioned timber modules. All load-bearing and non-load-bearing elements including the façade are modular. The R128 house is assembled by means of mortise-and-tendon joints and bolted joints. As a result, it is both easy to erect and dismantle, making it completely recyclable. There are no cables or pipes embedded in the walls. All supply and disposal systems as well as wiring is housed in metal ducts which run along the façades and are built into the floor and ceiling structures.

The R128 house produces no emissions and is entirely self-sufficient in its energy requirements. The electrical energy needed to operate the mechanical ventilation system and heat pump is supplied by the solar cell panels installed on the roof. This system uses the public electricity grid as a zero-loss energy store by feeding into it surplus energy and tapping it when there is an energy shortfall.

Using advanced smart technology, the house is devoid of switches, door handles, and other such fittings normally associated with comfortable residential living. Various functions in the house are controlled using non-touch sensors, voice control, or touch screens. Operations such as controlling lights, opening and closing windows, watering the garden and setting room temperatures use especially developed house control software. Activation is by means of touch screens provided on each floor and in the guest annex.

Bathrooms and toilets feature reflecting photocell units permitting a swipe of the hand to control opening and closing of doors and the flushing of toilets. Showers and washbasins also have non-touch controls.

The refrigerator has a concealed microwave sensor that responds to close-up hand movements to open and close the door.

The completely glazed building has triple glass panels. The heat energy radiated into the building by the sun is absorbed by water-filled ceiling panels and transferred to a heat store which provides warmth for the building in the winter by reversing the heat exchanging process. In this mode, the ceiling panels become radiators and no additional heating is needed. Another important ingredient of the climate management of House R128 is the mechanical ventilation system which controls the air flow and allows heat to be recovered from the exhaust air. Fresh air is injected at a single point on each floor and exhausted via the sanitary modules. To utilize the almost constant temperature of the subsoil as a heat source and heat store for preheating or precooling the fresh air supply, the exhausted air is blown through a heat exchanger located in the ground below the foundation of the house. The temperature inside the house can be selected separately for each floor.

Aluminum ceiling panels are clipped to the ceilings. These panels incorporate lights,

Left, east elevation at dusk with view of free-standing bathtub lower left. Following pages, a view of the north elevation with the suspended bridge that provides access to the main entrance of the house.

and acoustically absorbent surfaces as well as the heating
and cooling system consisting
of water-filled copper pipe coils.

All pipes and cables for
electricity, water, communication systems, and waste water
are run in folded aluminum
ducts along the inside of the
façades. This allows each function to be connected at any
point simply by opening the
appropriate duct. The free-
standing bathtub for example,
can be connected anywhere,
thanks to this flexible installa-
tion system.

The four-story staircase
as well as some areas not covered with ceiling panels create
continuous vertical spaces. The
absence of internal partitions
coupled with the all-glass
façade provide a visual continu-
ty between the horizontal,
internal, and external spaces.

One lives not so much in
House R128 but in a space that
is enclosed in a transparent,
high performance envelope.

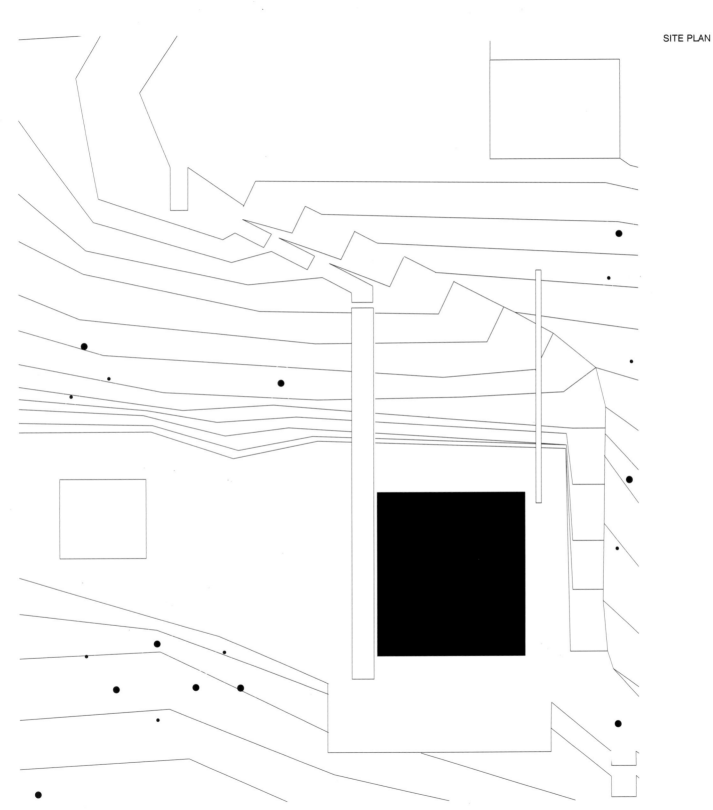

20 House R128

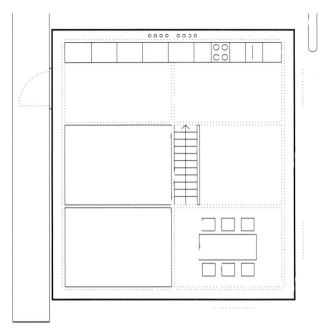

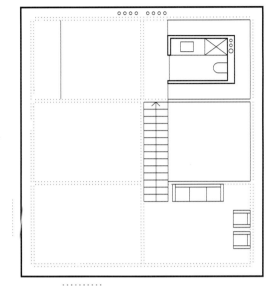

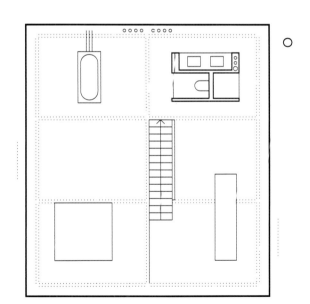

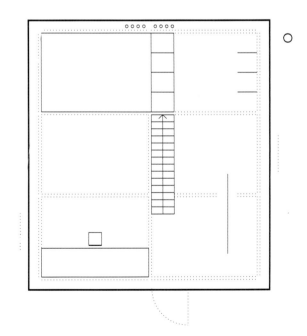

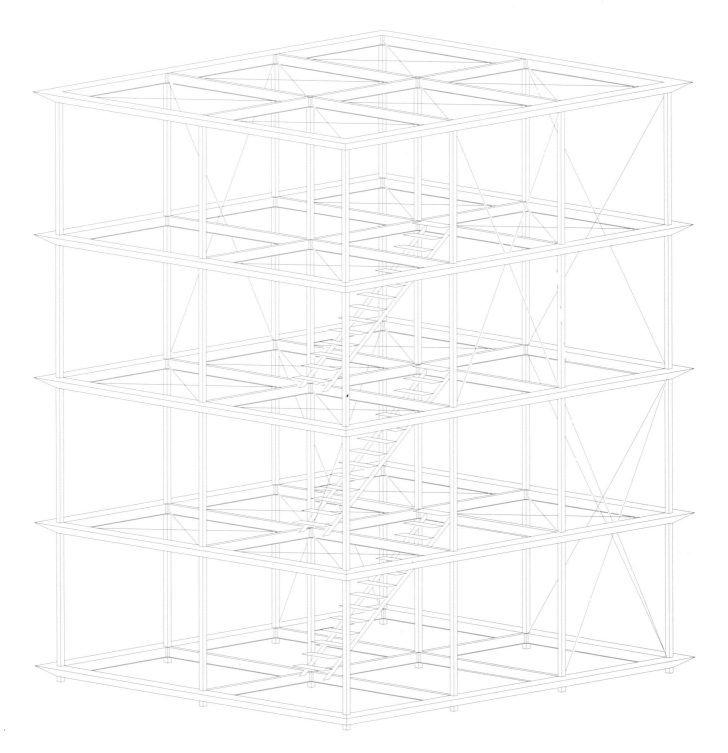

22 House R128

ELEVATIONS

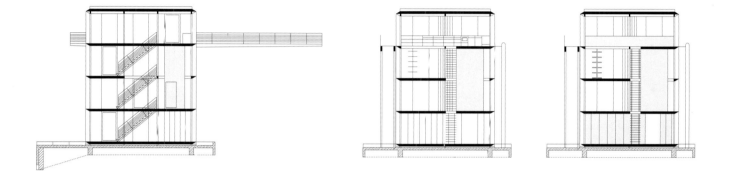

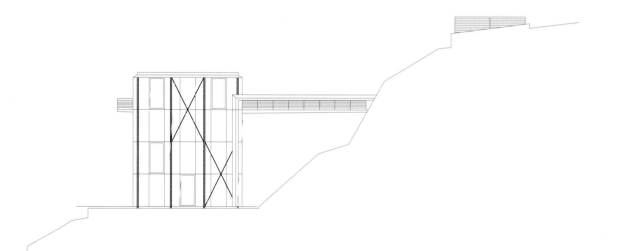

26 House R128

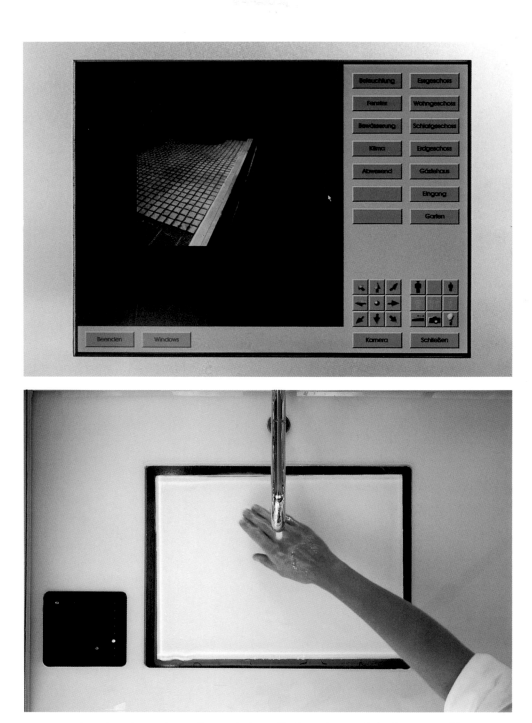

Previous pages, view from the east entrance gate showing the solar cell panels installed on the roof. Left, top and bottom, the guest annex as seen from the grounds and from the free-standing bath tub, respectively. Above, a sanitary module on the second floor. Top, house control software on one of the many touch screens in the house; a sensor-controlled wash basin.

Left, the exterior of the sanitary module with wash basins. Above, the sanitary module on the second floor.

Above, a view from the top floor entrance hall with the living area below. The heating and cooling panels are visible in the ceiling. Right, a detail of the staircase.

Left, each floor contains electronically-controlled hinged windows of the same dimensions as the fixed glazing. Above left, a detail of the façade and loadbearing structure. Above, the kitchen.

Left, dining area with living area below. Above, dining area. Following pages, view over the city of Stuttgart at dusk.

Eric Cobb Architects
Seattle, Washington

The site on the lakeshore in the Cascade Mountain Range was selected for its unique character, year around recreational opportunities, and proximity to Seattle. The topography is extremely steep, sloping down continuously from the road to the water dropping 54 feet over 126 feet in distance. In the winter, the average snowfall is ten feet.

Most of the adjacent shoreline is crowded with tall fir and cedar trees, with the exception of a few developed lots virtually all trees

have been cleared. In contrast, this house uses trees as a spatial asset. Instead of clear-cutting the trees, the house positions occupiable spaces high within the tree branches, allowing a line of trees to be a thin, selectively pruned veil between the house and the lake.

The house is configured in three parts: a box on top, a narrow two-story slab at the bottom, and a lightweight cantilevered shelf between the two. Entry and circulation are routed around, over, beneath and through the parts.

The top box contains a two-car garage with elevator, mudroom and storage below. A concrete deck warps to meet the sloping driveway. An exterior stair leads down to the entry, which is the space between the box and the shelf.

The two-story base or "sleeping bar" allows for 12 sleeping spaces. The bar is thin, stretching the spaces to maximize lake exposure and minimize the excavation for the foundation heel cut. The bedroom bar is 9 feet wide at the east end, tapering to 20 feet in depth in the middle, and then narrowing to 13 feet wide at the west. It contains four bedrooms (two connected by a climbing wall), a kids bunk cabin, two bathrooms, two built-in daybeds and a built-in hall bunk.

The third floor or "living shelf" is rotated and extended off the sleeping bar to position and orient the living area for views. This move also creates an exterior roof deck above a portion of the sleeping bar. This shelf is entirely open, with a galley kitchen defining the living space on one side and dining area on the other. The dining table anchors this floor with meals, games, and projects. The living space furniture is built-in, allowing for maximum occupancy and additional sleeping opportunities (fold-out sofa bed and corner sofa). The living shelf is virtually all glass facing the lake.

The project was driven by intelligent clients who demanded "smart" design. The clients (he is a software entrepreneur, she is a teacher) were interested in smart, interesting solutions—not just in wiring and hardware. They challenged the design team for solutions and inventions that went far beyond conventional architecture, design, and construction practice. The solutions needed to resolve multiple conditions and needs offer the unexpected, and appear simple, even "low-tech". In this project, "smart" meant solving a problem, then going for much more.

The solutions were to become more than a restatement of the problem.

The search for solutions and opportunities required a very fluid design process, allowing for major design shifts and changes deep into the design and even construction phases of work, without disrupting the project schedule. Late in the design process, the architects were asked to consider a "climbing wall" in the house. By lengthening the base of the house 4 feet, the climbing wall was constructed to connect the two stacked kid's bedrooms, in effect making a two-story kids' bunk chamber, with its own internal circulation (via climbing grips and ropes).

A disappearing "bunk box" was designed in the upper bedroom. Two flush wood doors (one tall, one short) open to reveal a built-in bunk cabin. In addition to the steel access ladder, each bunk has its own hidden door accessing separate landings of the stair. The kids can go to their individual bunks directly from the stair, and visit each other via stair or ladder. On the stair side of the wall, the two bunk doors are disguised as a wooden panel with chalk trays.

The stair treads are supported by a 22-foot-tall chalk board on all sides. This makes the stair itself an ongoing art project as well as communication surface ("we're at the lake"..."Anna loves Harry"...).

A full-height rolling door with a magnetic lock conceals a small office adjacent to the master bedroom.

On the living shelf, beyond the cantilevered living space, an exterior metal grating catwalk extends the cantilever even further. The catwalk allows for enjoyment of the views as well as facilitating window washing. The bar grating surface minimizes accumulated snow loads, and minimizes shadow on the windows below.

A kitchen peninsula incorporates a bookcase and telephone cabinet on its end, a pull-out sofa on the opposite side (with the upper sofa back a recessed kitchen storage compartment), and map storage behind the lower section of the sofa.

Cabinetry throughout the house, while accommodating unusual geometries dictated by the site, creates surprising interior spaces for games, stereo equipment, and books.

The wiring systems were designed with two primary goals: to provide control and monitoring of the house when unoccupied, and to provide easy, intuitive operations by guests. The installed systems include an electric snow melt designed to minimize accumulated snow at the garage door and deck doors, and to maintain a path to the deck hot tub.

There are also two web cameras providing views of critical snow build-up areas on the house, showing potential problems if the snow melt system fails.

Lights can be programmed and controlled individually and notification is provided of any open doors or windows. The house's thermostats are also controlled by this system.

A single "all house" switch sets all house systems to either "occupied mode" or "unoccupied mode", making it very easy for a guest, unfamiliar with the house systems, to arrive and leave without disrupting the programmed systems.

The house is intelligent and inventive in its response to the site, organization of spaces, invention in detail, as well as its use of technology.

Sited on a steep slope, the top floor living area is rotated to take advantage of the views.

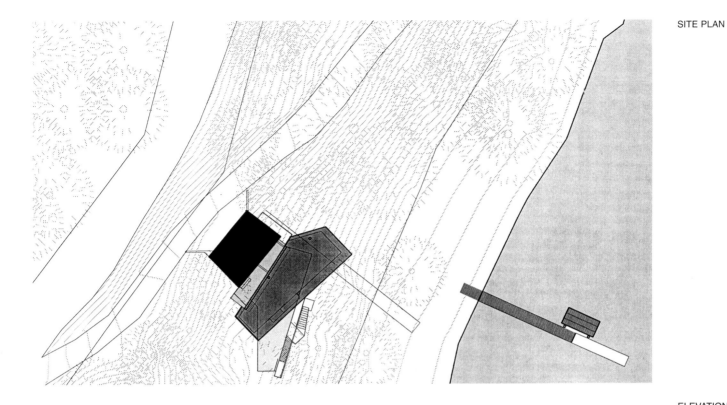

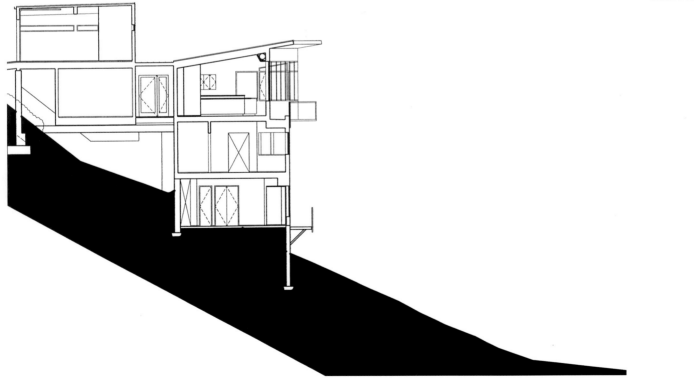

46 Lake House

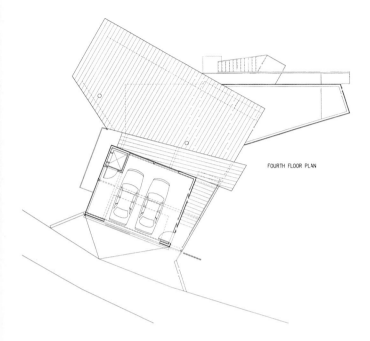

FOURTH FLOOR PLAN

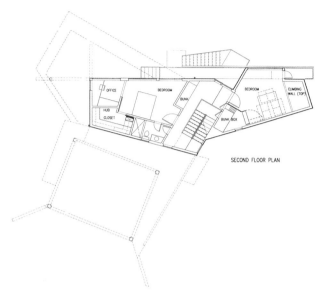

SECOND FLOOR PLAN

OFFICE BEDROOM BUNK BEDROOM CLIMBING WALL (TOP)

HUB

CLOSET BUNK BOX

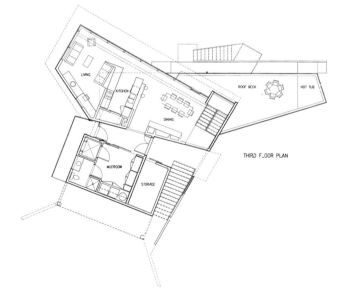

LIVING

KITCHEN ROOF DECK HOT TUB

DINING

MUDROOM

STORAGE

THIRD FLOOR PLAN

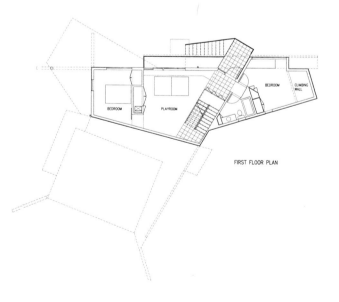

BEDROOM BEDROOM CLIMBING WALL

PLAYROOM

FIRST FLOOR PLAN

Above, the exterior metal grating catwalk is multi-functional, serving as an observation platform while making window washing easy on the top floor. Right, view of entry into third floor.

Above, the base of the climbing wall in the first floor bedroom. Clockwise from top right, the second floor bedroom at the top of the climbing wall; first floor bathroom; and view of main electrical panel and snow melt panels located in garage.

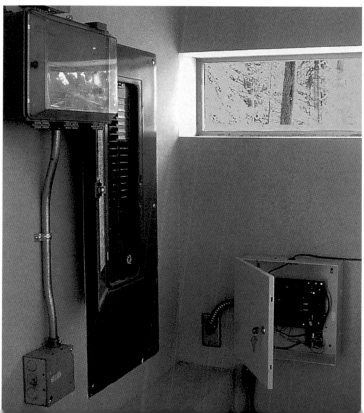
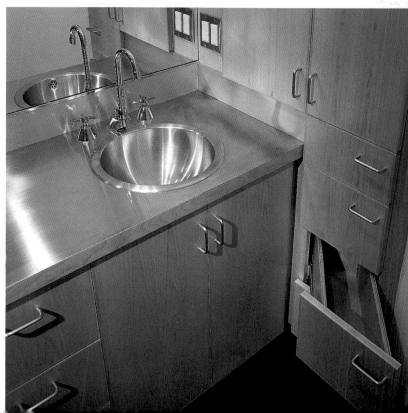

Above, a chalkboard lines the stairs, allowing a low-tech way to leave messages. Right, the stairwell at the second floor. A concealed bed is placed above the bookcase to the right.

Above, the kitchen. Right, the second floor bedroom "bunk box" with doors opened and closed.

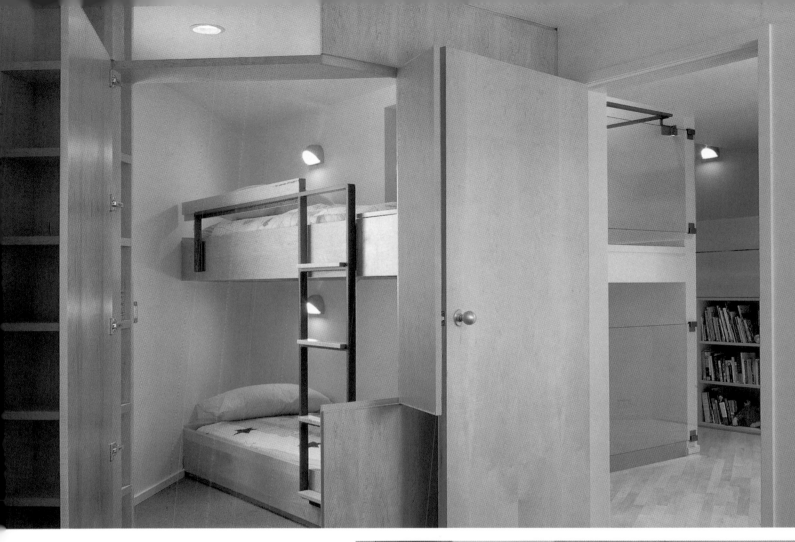

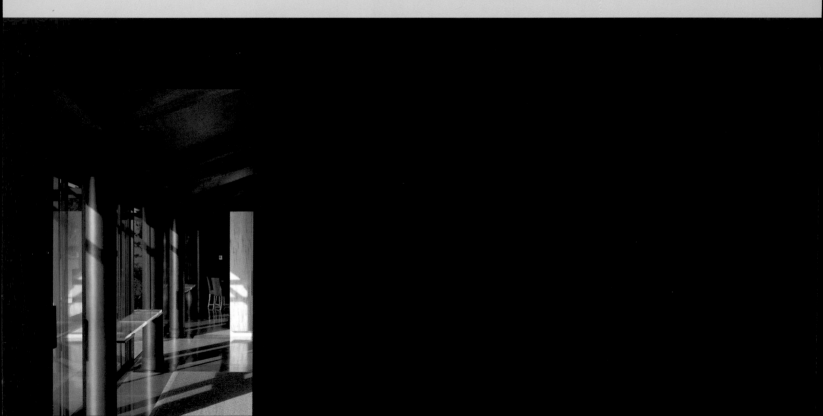

Courtyard House

This project involved a complete alteration and extensive additions

to an existing house originally designed in the 1960s. The owners

of this waterfront property wanted to create a family-focused

home. The result is a contemporary exploration of a formal court-

yard house. The house and garages sit on a terraced point of land

at the end of a dead-end drive. A landscaped overlook on the upper

terrace offers a glimpse of the house below and the lake beyond.

The house itself is situated 12 feet below the level of the garages

and is accessed via a gated walkway that descends alongside one of the garages. Beginning with the walkway, the house is revealed as a series of layered spaces with intermittent places of rest: people and water share a path through the site. A narrow slot in the entry walk reveals a stream of water that follows and flows beneath the walkway where it eventually cascades into a small pool in the entry courtyard.

The multi-level house is visually anchored to the ground by a lower level of integrally colored shot-crete concrete walls. These lower level masses were imagined as large stones found on the site and their earthy-brown coloring and texture fit comfortably into the landscape. The upper-levels where the bedrooms are located, were imaged as huts resting on the stones, and are clad in cedar siding and stained a warm brown. Metal railings are painted black. The landscape, which includes climbing vines to soften the structure of the house, merge the house into the landscape.

In plan, the house is designed as two, two-story masses separated by a low, transparent connecting pavilion. The pavilion physically and visu-

Previous pages, west façade highlighting the transparency of the central, glass living pavilion. Above, view of the glass pavilion with the private courtyard in the foreground.

60 Courtyard House

ally unites the courtyard to the lakeside terrace and to the lake through large sliding glass wall panels. The terraces, extensive glazing, external columns, and trellises serve to extend the architecture into the landscape of the site.

Electronically, the house relies on an umbrella system to integrate the four basic subsystems of the house: security, lighting, sun-shading, and audio visuals. The umbrella system allows all of the subsystems to be linked and provides infinite customization possibilities for the homeowner. The system can be operated and modified from anywhere in the world. Each room has a small, local system keypad that operates basic pre-planned lighting scenes. Wall mounted touch screens are placed in centralized locations throughout the house providing full systems access. Each of the centralized touch screens is designed to fit discreetly into the architecture and interior design of the house. The media room systems are controlled via handheld touch screen. A central control room houses all of the systems, with computer equipment racks for each of the source devices.

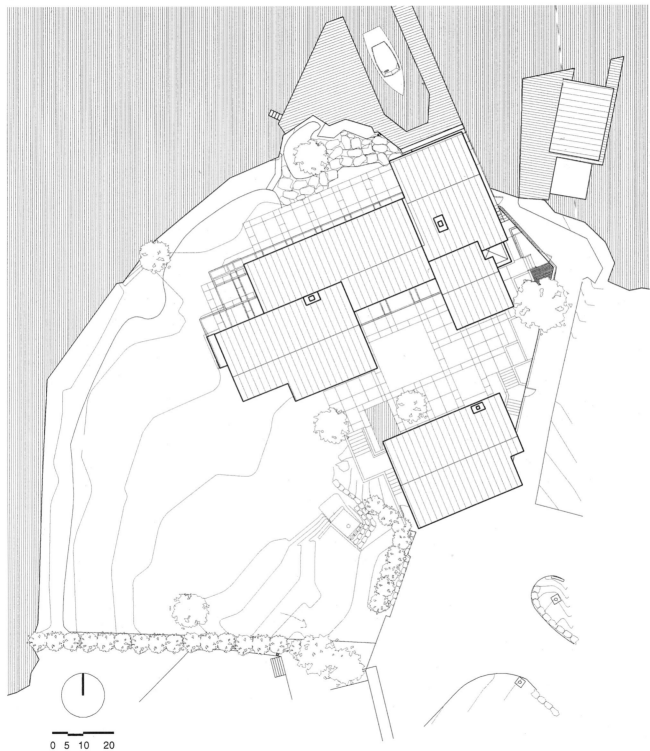

0 5 10   20

62 Courtyard House

STREET LEVEL PLAN

COURTYARD LEVEL PLAN

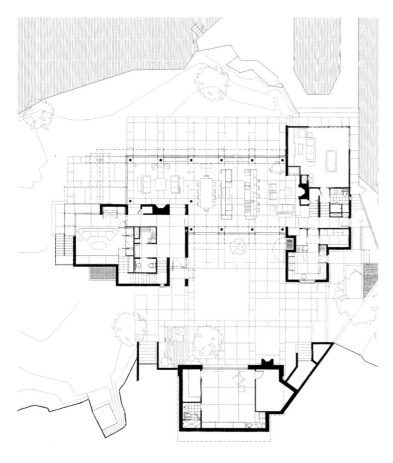

0 5 10 20

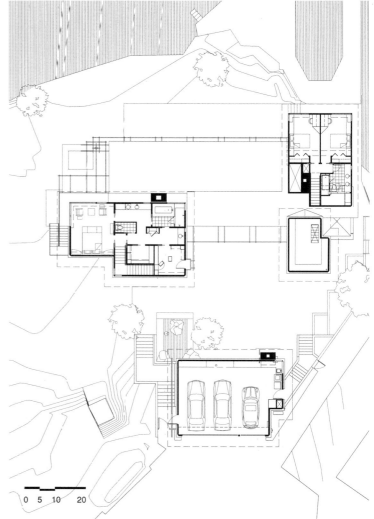

0 5 10 20

63

Above, looking north into the courtyard with a view of the two bedroom pavilions. Right, a view across the courtyard toward the guest pavilion with the garage above.

Above, a view looking north across the courtyard. The bronze doors conceal a barbeque. Right, the approach to the house as seen from the front door. The shifting entry sequence redirects the view of the visitor to visually experience the entire site. Water, which flows in a slotted runnel in the pathway, cascades into a small pool. Integrally colored, steel troweled shot-crete is used as the primary exterior material and is also used for some interior surfaces.

Left, view from dining room looking across fused glass dining table. Above left, the sliding doors to the media room. The doors are maple with bronze details. Above right, the media room featuring maple cabinetry.

Above, view from living room to the dining room. Right, view toward entry looking across living room.

Daly, Genik Architects
Los Angeles, California

At 1800 feet above sea level, the site for this 3000-square-foot

house is in the foothills surrounding Mt. Palomar in California over-

looking a 25-acre citrus and avocado ranch. The site is covered with

exposed granite boulders, decomposed granite shale, and underly-

ing granite monoliths. Citrus groves extend downward from the

site, and the Channel Islands off the Southern California coast are

visible to the west. The house replaces a ranch house that burned

in a wildfire a few years ago.

The client wanted a house without interior stairs that was easy to

maintain and economical to heat and cool. Sun shading and fire-resistant building materials were important considerations in the design and construction.

The house is organized as two wings of sleeping quarters—relatively opaque to the exterior—that flank a large living/dining area that is entirely glazed. These three building elements form a courtyard that opens to the grove below and the coastal view beyond. A swimming pool notches into one side of the courtyard.

The exterior of the two sleeping wings is sheathed in corrugated concrete board. Large openings to the courtyard are covered with bi-folding perforated metal panels. Sliding panels allow the sleeping quarters to open fully to the courtyard. The interior wall surfaces and ceiling are birch plywood.

The exterior surfaces of the building serve as the primary environmental conditioning scheme for the house, achieved through the refractory properties of the concrete board and in the reflective nature of the aluminum panels. These panels create large shaded areas immediately outside the main living space, allowing the house to remain open with-

out being exposed. They a so protect the large glass surfaces from direct sunlight.

The perforated aluminum panels are operated as large bi-folding doors on the north- and south-facing surfaces of the courtyard. On the east- and west-facing surfaces of the main spaces they are large operable awning panels that are adjustable. During the cooler months of the year, they are used to reflect sunlight onto the ceiling of the living/dining area.

Left and below, surrounded by granite terrain, the perforated aluminum panels adjust to protect the house from sun and wind.

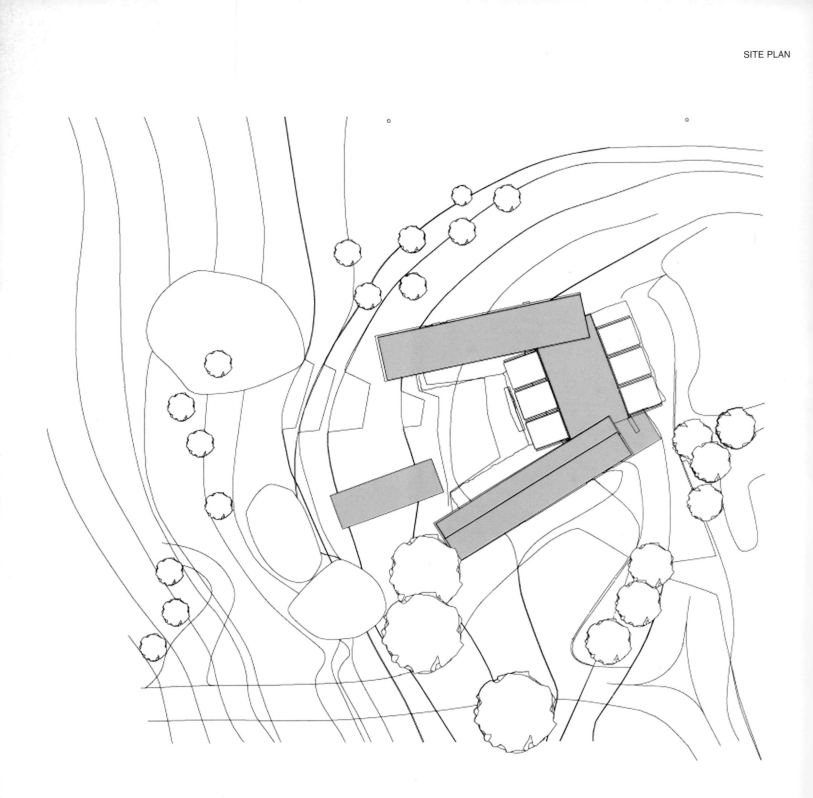

78 Valley Center

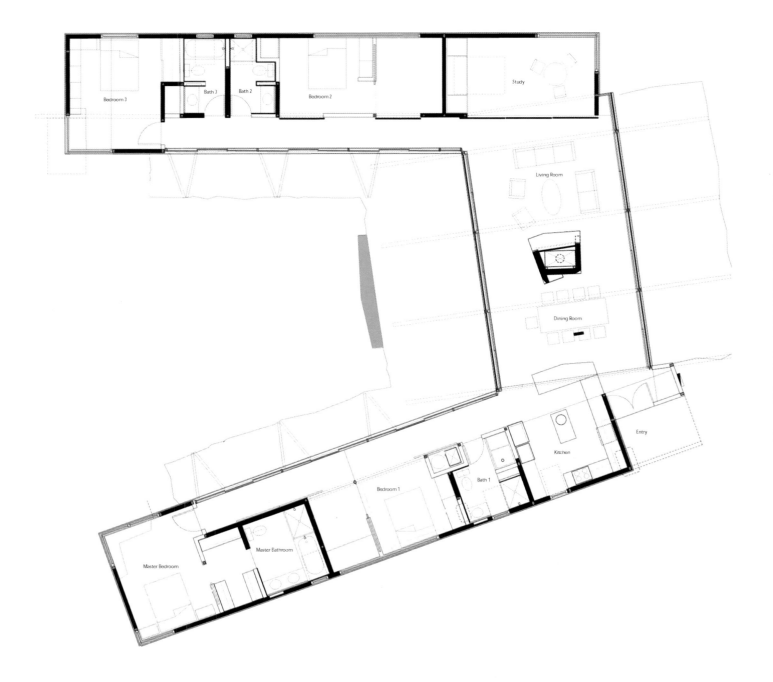

Bedroom 3

Bath 3

Bath 2

Bedroom 2

Study

Living Room

Dining Room

Entry

Kitchen

Bath 1

Bedroom 1

Master Bathroom

Master Bedroom

Left and above, the house embraces the courtyard and swimming pool.

Left and above, views of the fully glazed living/dining area that is flanked by the bedroom wings.

Left, large sliding panels enclose sleeping areas in alcoves off the glazed corridors. Above, exterior view of bedroom wing. Following pages, a view of perforated aluminum panels in the raised position.

Balance Associates, Architects
Seattle, Washington

This 1400-square-foot cabin is located in the mountains of north-

central Washington State on a south facing slope with views to the

south and east. Careful attention was given to the material selec-

tion for the house. These materials—logs, sawn beams, rough

formed concrete, and corrugated metal—reflect the untamed natu-

ral setting. The house is sided with wood that was salvaged from a

water irrigation ditch. The 2-by-12s used in framing have naturally

weathered over the last 60 years. They were cleaned and sealed

when they were installed. The roof purlins are lodge pole pine logs

that are from forest thinning.

The cabin was designed to take advantage of passive solar heating. The majority of the high performance glazing faces either south or east. The east facing glazing provides morning warming where even in the summer, nighttime lows often dip into the 30s. Large amounts of thermal mass were designed into the house to reduce diurnal temperature fluctuations. The roof is insulated to R-50 and the walls to R-23. As a result, energy use is significantly below code requirements for the area.

Two concrete walls form terraces upon which the two-level house rests. The lower terrace contains the living, dining, and kitchen areas all as one space. The upper concrete wall forms the back of the living area and creates a base for the upper terrace where two bedrooms and a bath are located. To connect the interior with the natural surroundings, all rooms have doors that open to the outside including the bath, which opens to an outdoor bath for use during the summer months.

Previous pages, left, and above, views of the house and garage from various elevations, in the winter and summer.

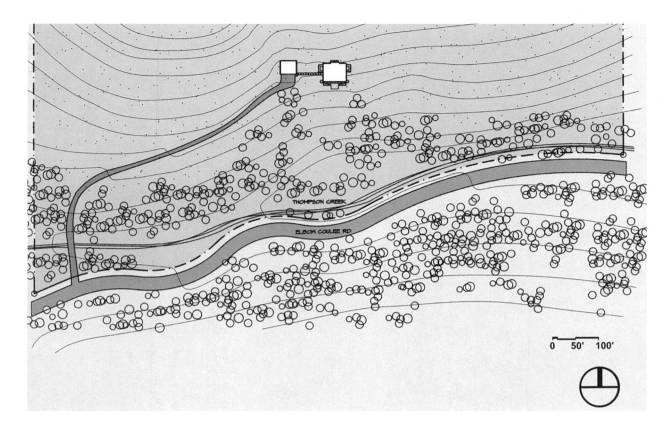

THOMPSON CREEK

ELBOW COULEE RD

0   50'   100'

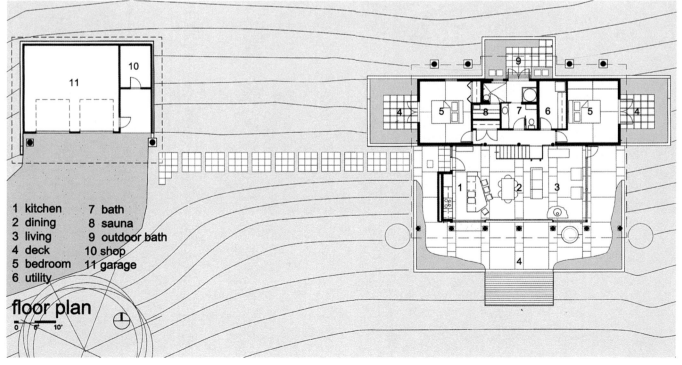

1 kitchen   7 bath
2 dining   8 sauna
3 living   9 outdoor bath
4 deck   10 shop
5 bedroom   11 garage
6 utility

floor plan

0   5'   10'

94 Cabin at Elbow Coulee

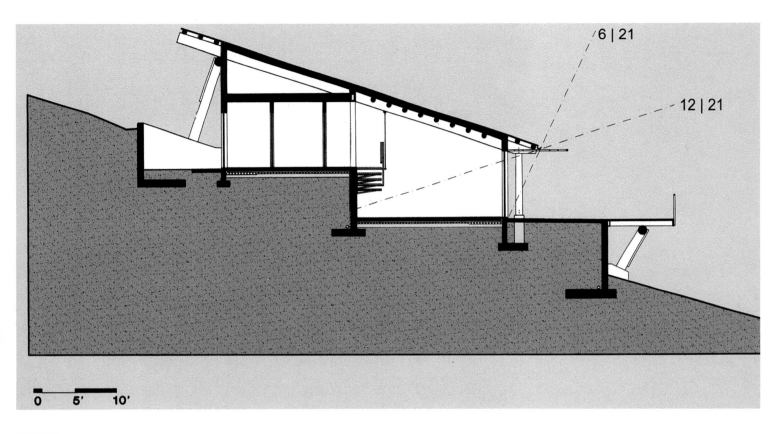

6 | 21

12 | 21

0   5'   10'

SECTION

SOUTH WALL SECTION

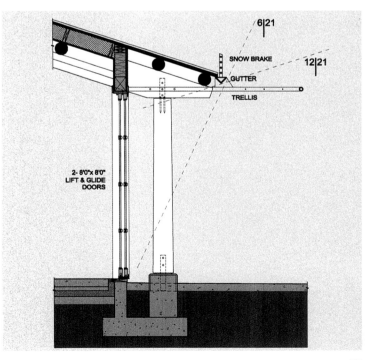

6|21

12|21

SNOW BRAKE

GUTTER

TRELLIS

2- 8'0"x 8'0"
LIFT & GLIDE
DOORS

Left, south elevation and above, south patio looking east. Following pages, view of the living/dining room.

Previous pages, views of dining and kitchen areas. Left, the master bedroom looking northeast. Above, bathroom looking northwest and a view from the outdoor bath looking in.

SMART MATERIALS

Lorcan O'Herlihy Architects

The house sits on a sloping, irregularly shaped ancient alluvial bluff

in the Santa Monica Mountains. The double residential hillside lot is

approximately 19,000 square feet with southwest views towards

the ocean and the Santa Monica mountains.

The project started as a 3200-square-foot addition to a 1400-

square-foot wood-sided house in the Pacific Palisades, California.

The commission grew in scope, requiring the demolition of all but

the second floor of the existing house, and eventually engulfing the original structure. At the outset of the project the architect undertook a study of hillside houses. The dominant approach offered a choice between "adhering" and "hovering", between anchoring the building to the slope, or suspending the structure above it. It became clear that the solution was a combination of the two. The existing structure adhered to the slope and remained so. Where new architectural elements were added, a suggestion of suspension was accomplished by extending the overhangs and wrapping the windows around corners.

The residence attempts to create an ensemble of living volumes which engage the natural virtues of the site. The existing, inward looking house was oblivious to its beautiful wooded site; the intrigue of the project was going to be its detailing and the differentiating between its diverse building components, including glass, steel windows, and smooth troweled plaster. This is apparent in the new master bedroom wing with its opaque lower-level suite and the library above it. The new bedroom/library wing reaches out over the descending hillside, with the prismatic library volume on top completely enveloped beneath the broad

canopy of existing pines and surrounding landscaped view. A translucent linear cast-glass structural glazing system was used for the library and bridge connection to the main house. A simple concept of self supporting glass channels within an extruded metal perimeter frame permits a cost effective cladding system adaptable to almost any building design. The linear glass channel is formed through computer controlled furnaces, consistently producing glass of the highest quality and accurate dimensions. The U-shaped configuration of the glass provides an inherent strength within the channel against lateral loading, allowing the system to be installed at high level or large unit lengths, without incorporating additional vertical or horizontal supports. This glass was also used in the office above the garage.

       With the juxtaposition of varied surfaces, proliferation of entrances, and play of spaces, elevations, observation points, volumes, and materials, the expanded house approaches the complexity of a city.

Previous pages, the bedroom wing with the roof terrace library. Above, the channel glass library with bridge to main house.

View of library from main entry.

110 Freund/Koopman Residence

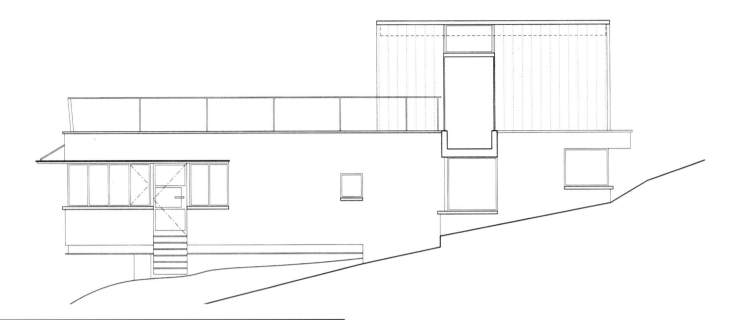

MODEL

112 Freund/Koopman Residence

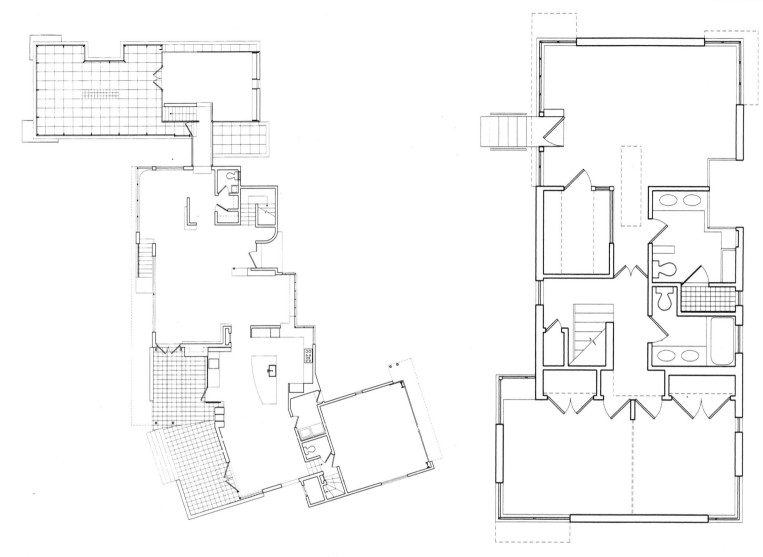

Left, an exterior view of the channel glass bridge to the library. Above, view of garden and trellis leading to the living room. The master bedroom wing is to the left.

Above, channel glass forms the walls of the bridge to the roof-terrace library. Right, stairway to the library.

Above, the dining room, and right, the kitchen.

Master bedroom and master bath.

Francois deMenil Architect
New York, New York

The Shorthand House seeks to reintroduce basic spatial aware-

ness and potentiality to the suburban domestic environment by

translating the linguistic rules of shorthand into a flexible system of

symbolic architectural references. The use of shorthand as a con-

ceptual model was suggested by the client's extensive use of the

speedwriting technique in her work.

In the Shorthand House, public rooms are not defined by walls but

by symbols. Traditional "rooms" are reduced to the components

that most clearly distill and represent their function. These elements

serve as symbolic references to potential spatial boundaries within an open living space. The symbols can be joined and related in a variety of ways to achieve differing spatial configurations.

The continuous living space at the ground floor provides a flexible framework for manipulating the interior into a variety of discrete spaces as needed. Within the overall spatial continuity of the building envelope, shorthand "rooms" exist when needed and fold away when not required. Spatial phraseograms link spaces with closely related functions and domestic associations. Each floor comprises a series of phraseograms for living.

The rectilinear volume was chosen for its spatial familiarity and ease of construction. The box's deceptively simple exterior acts counterpoint to the wealth of potential spatial conditions latent within it.

Because the occupant must physically engage the house in order to alter the spatial condition, he or she is, of necessity, simultaneously engaged in understanding the meaning and experience of space and architecture.

Previous pages, the west façade of the house showing the entrance. Left and above, the east façade overlooking the court-yard. The shutters on the second floor allow for privacy and light control while the narrow band of windows above remain uncovered.

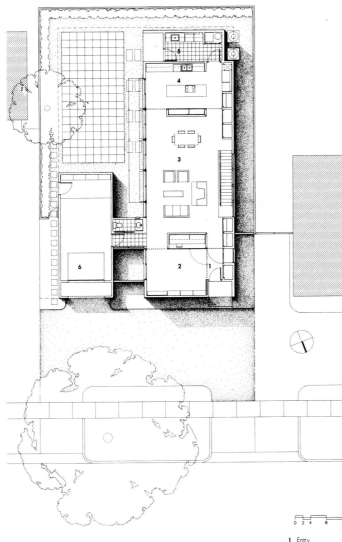

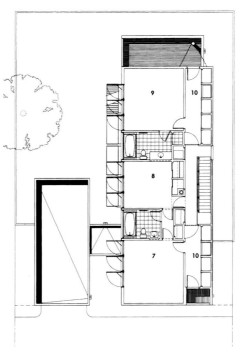

1 Entry
2 Shorthand Foyer/Study
3 Living/Dining Area
4 Kitchen/Shorthand Pantry
5 Laundry
6 Garage

7 Bedroom
8 Bedroom/Shorthand Sitting Room
9 Master Bedroom
10 Shorthand Dressing Room/Corridor

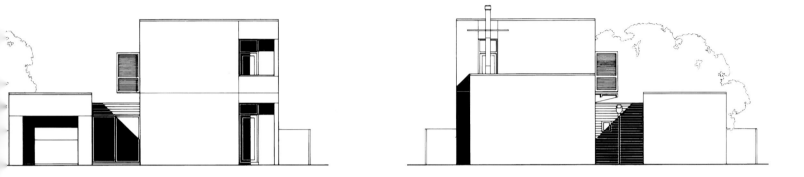

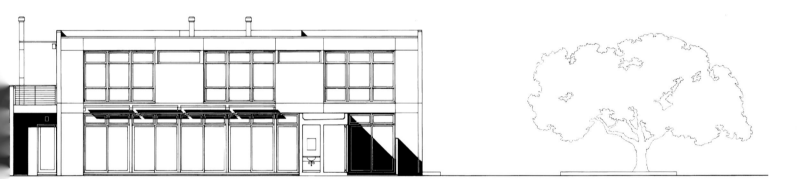

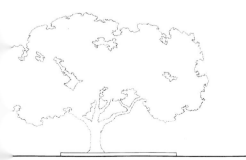

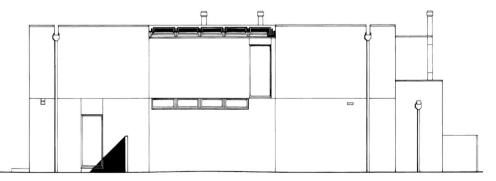

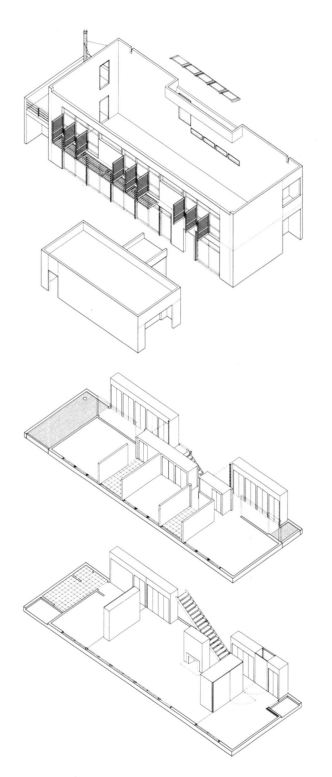

130 Shorthand House

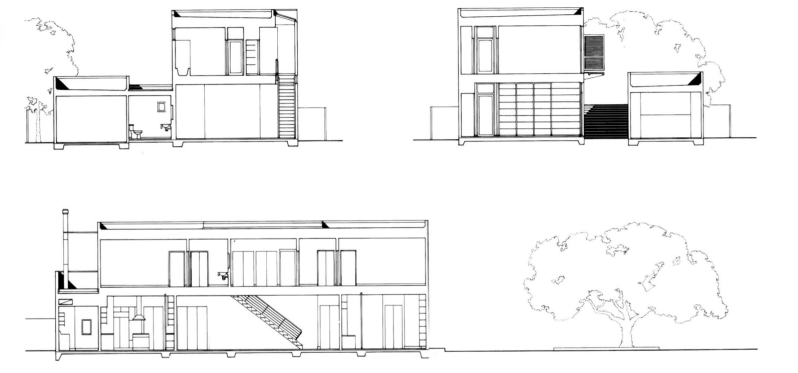

Left and above, the heart and soul of the Shorthand House is the "shorthand study" shown in the closed and open positions, respectively. In the open position, it becomes a private retreat from the rest of the house. When open, the first floor is like a large open loft. The kitchen can similarly be closed off, with the kitchen pantry, visible on the left, operating much like the study.

Left, a view from the kitchen along the transparent east wall towards the study. Above, the kitchen.

Above and above right, a narrow band of windows the thickness of the floor sandwich provide light along the "opaque" side of the house. Skylights provide additional light for this side of the house and the staircase. Rignt, the master bedroom. Following pages, a view from the courtyard at dusk when the transparency of the house is most apparent.

Isolating the hillside house as a building type is very important for

architectural discourse. Sloping sites offered California modernists,

Wright, Schindler, Neutra, Lautner, and others, the opportunity to

invent new forms, transforming the house. Continuing in this tradi-

tion the Lexton/MacCarthy site offered wonderful west-facing views

of Los Angeles and suggested a formal strategy of an abstract geo-

metrical form conceived as a play of positive and negative volumes.

The house sits on a steeply sloping lot in Silverlake. The deep vertical section of the site did not lend itself to an easy solution. Working with the structural engineer Paul Franceschi, the siting of the house, carport, and stair was conceived as a "straight dislocation". The carport "breaks away" from the house with its path traced by a connecting stairway. Retaining walls, excavation, and site grading are typically a major portion of the construction cost for hillside houses. The building pad elevation and siting were considered to minimize the heights of retaining walls and amount of grading.

The program was for a 2000-square-foot house with a carport. Given this limited size, the primary floor is conceived as a plan, which allows for programmatic flexibility. The second story houses the master bedroom suite. The section of the second floor traces an area on the first floor that houses the kitchen, stair, bathroom, and closet. The building fenestration on the west wall at the living room recedes and the fenestration at the core of the house reinforces the vertical line through the glu-laminated columns. The house is wrapped in 1-by-6 Douglas fir horizontal siding which floats away from the structure with 2-by-2-inch vertical spacers. The siding is

stained blue on the second floor.

The internal plan and distribution of the program is suggested in the treatment of the exterior skin. The idea of the house is to establish a horizontal layer on the primary floor and vertical volume on the second floor.

A new vocabulary for wood structures was proposed. The formal simplicity allows for a greater focus on materials, proportions, and details. The abstract geometrical forms stripped of superfluous detailing reinforce the modernist reticence, but is mediated through the use of wood surfaces which play with the California light. Frank Lloyd Wright's Usonian houses were used as a point of departure. As opposed to the idea that a building should reveal its construction at first glance this solution blurs that criterion and allows the skin to wrap structure, glass, concrete or ply-

Previous pages and right, views of the front of the house from the street below. Above, the house as seen from the courtyard garden.

Above, the curtain wall as seen from the street. Right, an exterior detail of 1-by-6-inch pine slats.

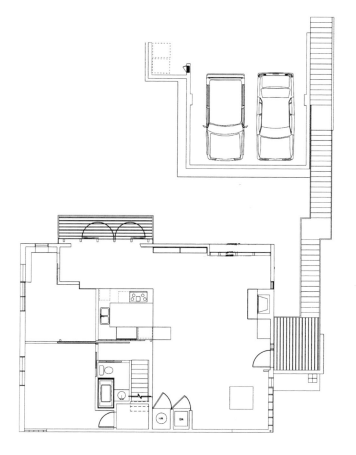
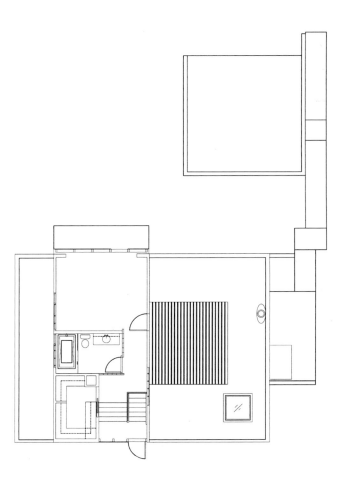

148 Lexton/MacCarthy Residence

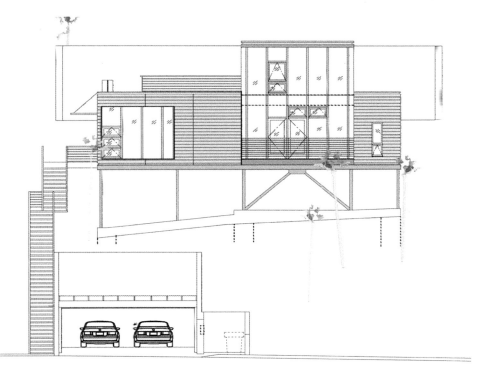

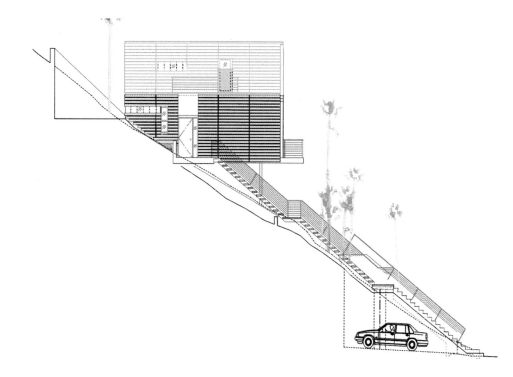

Left, stairwell with channel glass walls surrounding the master bathroom. Above, view of office with acrylic slider. Following pages, view of open living area on the main level.

Above and right, the master bath with channel glass walls separating it from the master bedroom.

Above, views of the living area and master bedroom. Right, the exterior slatted wall is revealed through the window in the living room. Following pages, a door leads to the master bedroom from the roof deck.

Lita Recio

From the beginning, the architects wanted to create a home that

interlocked with the landscape, so that each room would have max-

imum light as well as a direct connection to the site and views of

the surrounding mountains. The integration of the house with the

site is in contrast to the prevailing model of a large country property

(in this case, 10,000 square feet). The design for the house is a

series of parallel walls that define spatial volumes which interlock

to enable movement between them. The house was oriented so

that the Sneffils Range would be seen between parallel walls, along their axis, and the Ophir Needles appear through the openings in the walls.

The Colorado house is located in a meadow and the clients wanted the views to be an essential part of the overall experience of the house. A 13-by-17 mile computer model was constructed to precisely position the house on the site and to locate windows to maximize the view.

A custom-designed "rain screen" wall is made of corten steel shingles. The design of this wall and the detailing of the shingles were developed in conjunction with metal fabricators. The shingle pattern varies. The walls on the north side have a pattern that is slightly different from the south face walls. The difference in patterns is achieved through small adjustments in the overlap of the shingles making one surface appear static while the other appears to have movement. The shingles rest on sandblasted concrete foundations. At certain points the shingles slip into the house, accentuating the relationship between inside and outside.

The parallel walls are covered with corten steel. The house is conceived as a series of landscape walls that frame the views from within the house.

168 Colorado House

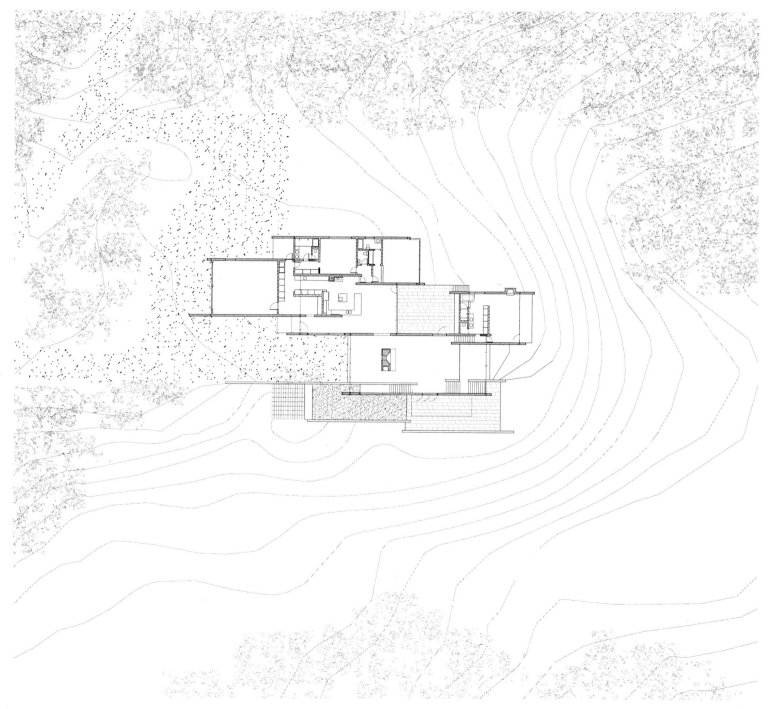

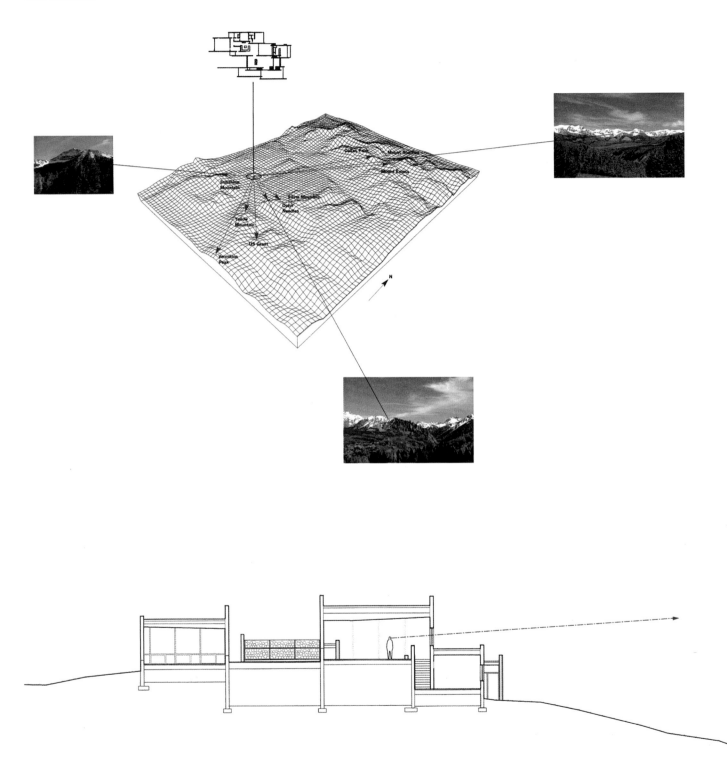

170 Colorado House

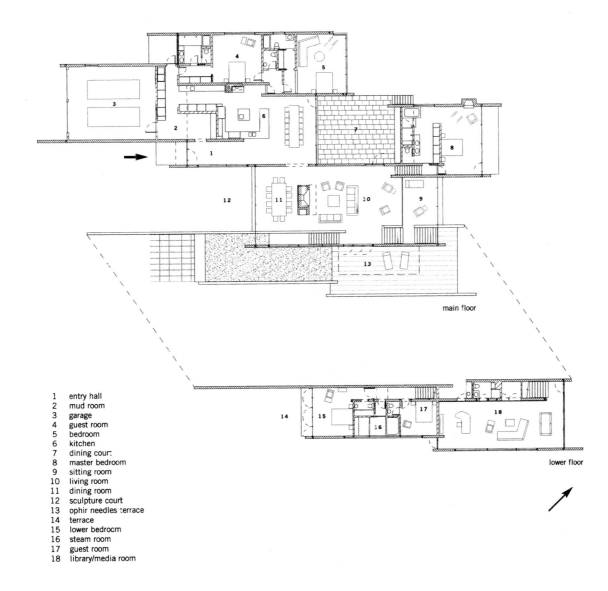

main floor

lower floor

1 entry hall
2 mud room
3 garage
4 guest room
5 bedroom
6 kitchen
7 dining court
8 master bedroom
9 sitting room
10 living room
11 dining room
12 sculpture court
13 ophir needles terrace
14 terrace
15 lower bedroom
16 steam room
17 guest room
18 library/media room

0'   20'

Left, a view from the living room to the magnificent scenery beyond. Above, the master bath.

Above, the kitchen with a view of one of the parallel walls jutting into the landscape. Right, a view from the living room down the stairs to the family room below.

Bohlin Cywinski Jackson
Seattle, Washington

Photography: Karl Backus, Ben Benschneider, Fred Housel

This 2100-square-foot house stretches along a narrow sloping site

with views of an arboretum and the distant Cascade Mountains.

The building was positioned to preserve two major trees, a

Madrona and a large Deodar cedar.

The owners worked in close collaboration with the design team to

achieve an architecture that pays particular attention to the nature

of building materials and the expression of the way things are put

together. The result is a space that is lively yet calm, with bold use

of basic building materials such as wood, plywood, concrete, and steel.

The essentially open layout includes a master bedroom that overlooks the double-height living room, two offices that can be used as guest rooms, and such refinements as a mail-sorting nook shielded by a small sliding barn door.

A spine of steel channels and columns extends the entire length of the house, projecting through its face to support two private decks. Wood studs were left exposed or revealed behind plywood panels. Screens of cedar framing and polycarbonate glazing stretch along the edges of the carport, extending into the building and, combined with the steel spine, serve to pull one through to the long views. A tracery of horizontal flashing bands and fasteners gives a delicate pattern to the house's exterior.

As a finished composition, the house reveals the particular nature of its site, of its owners, and of the materials with which it is made.

Previous pages, on the north elevation, polycarbonate glazing peels back from a cedar frame allowing views from the office deck while screening the carport. Left and above, the house opens to the east taking advantage of the views. A series of multilevel decks tuck themselves between existing trees and shrubbery providing a sense of seclusion in a dense Seattle neighborhood.

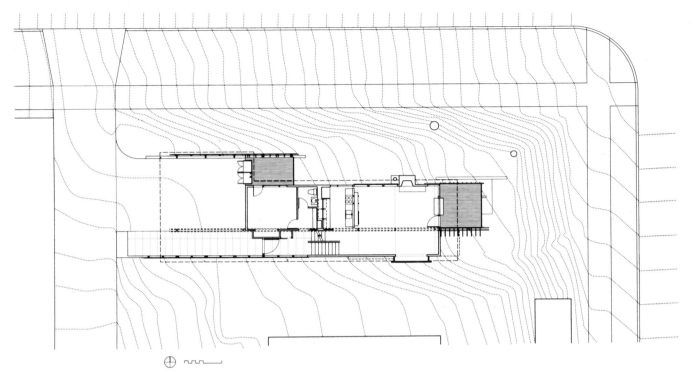

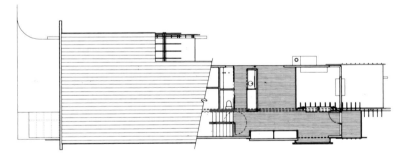

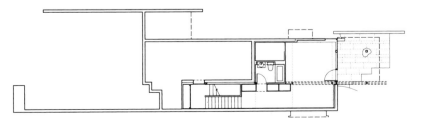

182 Gosline House

Above, the entrance as seen from the garage with polycarbonate glazing on the right allowing filtered light into the space.

NORTH ELEVATION

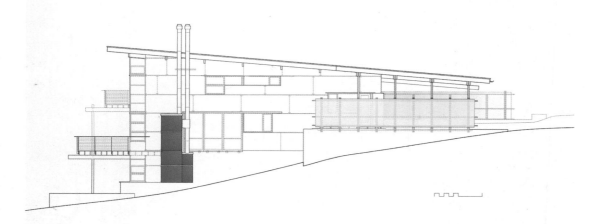

SOUTH ELEVATION

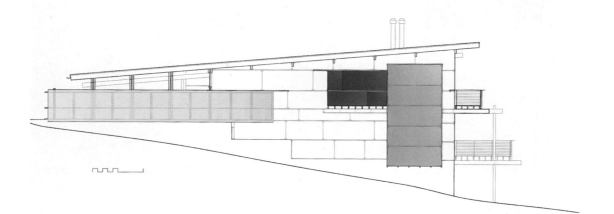

184 Gosline House

Above, view of model from northeast. Right, a view of model with roof removed.

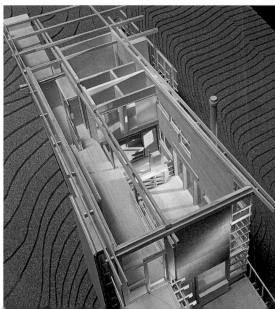

Above, exposed wood framing, colored concrete floors, and steel are carefully blended throughout the house. Right, a series of tall corner windows frame a Deodar cedar, one of the largest trees in the neighborhood. Following pages, an open plan links the living room to the kitchen giving a sense of spaciousness to this 2100-square-foot house.

Above, steel plates slip past maple plywood panels at the living room fireplace. Right, a view of the staircase.

Above, view from master bedroom. Articulated maple bookshelves double as the guard rail.